Meditations on Design

MEDITATIONS ON DESIGN

Reinventing Your Home with Style and Simplicity

JOHN WHEATMAN

Photography by David Wakely

Produced by Sharon Smith and Barbara Stevenson

CONARI PRESS

ISBN: 1-57324-823-1

Cover and Book Design: Sharon Smith
Author Photo: David Wakely
Composition: Deborah Reinerio

Excerpt from *A House is A Home* © 1978 Mary Anne Hoberman reprinted by permission of Penguin Putnam Inc.

Library of Congress Cataloging-in-Publication Data

Wheatman, John.
    Meditations on design : reinventing your home with style and simplicity / John Wheatman.
        p. cm.
    ISBN 1-57324-823-1 PB
    ISBN 1-57324-192-X HC
    1. Interior decoration—United States—History—20th century—Themes, motives.
2. Interior decoration—Themes, motives. I. Title.

NK2004 .W48 2000
747—dc21
                                                            99–042091

First paperback edition 2002.
Printed in Singapore.

02 03 04 TWP 10 9 8 7 6 5 4 3 2 1

To my wife, Mary,
who won't let me
bring another chair
into our house!

I would like to thank Sharon Smith and David Wakely for their unending enthusiasm in taking this book from a dream to a reality. Thank you also to Barbara Stevenson for capturing my voice.

I would also like to thank my students, customers, and clients. It has been my pleasure to serve you, learn from you, and to build with you creative spaces within which to house your memories. I would especially like to thank Pat and Rodney Baker, Louise Burns, Judy and Mel Croner, John Demergasso, Joyce and George DeMott, George Doubleday II, Barbara and James Fetherston, Betty and Jim Kelso, Ellen and Joerg Michelfelder, Dr. and Mrs. Richard Moomjian, Anne and Victor Parachini, Katherine and Robert Renfield, David and Yvonne Rich, Spaulding Taylor, and Brent Wallis for generously allowing us to photograph their homes.

Thank you also to all the talented designers, craftsmen, and professionals I have had the privilege of working with over the years. Thank you to my dedicated office staff for smoothing out the rough edges and a special thank you to Bill Weir for his lifelong friendship and counsel.

—JOHN WHEATMAN

The book producers gratefully acknowledge the significant contributions of Carolyn Miller and Kenneth Caldwell to the creative direction of this project in its early stages. We also offer warm thanks to Mary Jane Ryan, Jenny Collins, Deborah Reinerio, Diane Buzzini, and Joan Olson for their assistance with editing and production, and to Beth Roy for overall support.

MEDITATIONS ON DESIGN

REINVENTING YOUR HOME
It Takes an Open Mind and an Adventurous Heart

> If I were asked to say what is at once the most important production of Art
> and the thing most to be longed for, I should answer, "a beautiful house."
> —WILLIAM MORRIS

One of my favorite teachers in college, Ed Rossbach, taught me the single most important lesson I've ever learned about design. "Cultivate the mind of a three-year-old," he commanded. To a three-year-old, everything is new, and every day is an adventure. Young children don't spend a lot of time thinking about what other people expect of them; they don't enter into situations with preformed ideas of what's going on and what should happen. They have open minds and adventurous hearts. And they know how to have fun! Ever since that day many years ago, I have tried to wake up every morning as a three-year-old. I encourage you to try it yourself.

An open mind is essential to good home design. Yet I often find that people come to the project of designing or redecorating their homes with their minds full of ideas about what they should do or not do. When I have persuaded them to clear their minds of these preconceptions, my clients begin to find our work together much more creative and fulfilling. So I would ask every reader of this book—as a favor to yourself—to reject the common myths about interior design.

For instance, many people believe that no one but a design professional can decorate a house. They feel that they must either copy schemes they see in magazines or hire an interior designer to make their homes look "tasteful." The truth is, just as no two people are alike, no two houses are alike. If you point to a picture in a magazine and say, "I want this for my home," you have skipped over the most important phase of the design process. You must go beyond how your room looks and begin to analyze who you are and how you use that room. Only when you've figured out how to be comfortable doing the things you do in that space can you move on to the question of how it should look.

Similarly, I have often encountered the notion that interior design consists of essentially casting out what you have and buying everything new. In fact, some of my most satisfying projects have not involved the purchase of any additional furnishings. I always begin by editing what is already in place. I help people discard the items that don't work and organize the ones that remain so that everything comes together and makes sense—functionally, visually, and financially. Sometimes that's all that's necessary.

Many people also believe that you must always keep resale value in mind when remodeling or furnishing your home. (No wonder they approach the task full of insecurity and dread!) If you arrange your space for someone else—a nameless, faceless prospective buyer—you are cheating yourself out of the comfort of a home that meets your needs now. You may also be creating something that is bland and boring. Consider the difference between appointing a space that won't offend anyone and composing a room as a reflection of who you are and what you love. I think the latter is more exciting.

Another common mistake is to think of a house or apartment as only an interior space. I believe in stepping back and starting with what leads up to a home. If you have a house, then you need to look at not only the interior space, but also the trees and shrubbery, and your neighbor's property. If you have an apartment or a flat, you need to start with the hallway outside your front door: What do you want it to do and how do you want it to look, as an approach to your home? If you have a garden, how are you going to bring the outside in? Your home is your shelter, and that protection begins with the transition from the outside world.

Finally, people often come to me with the expectation that we will "do" their homes together and then the job will be "done." But who you are and what you want to say about yourself is continually changing. How you live and what you can afford also changes over time: You start a family, or your children grow up and leave to live on their own; you take up a new hobby or develop a new collecting interest. A good home changes and evolves with you—a good home is never done.

I was fortunate to grow up with parents who were masters at the arts of living well and entertaining generously. When my family built a new house, my room—which I helped to plan—became a popular meeting place for my high school circle. The joy of entertaining friends in my own space at an early age inspired me to observe my parents closely and discern the secrets of a good life. In every place I've lived since then, it has been my deep delight to re-create the generosity and grace of my boyhood home.

Once I began to study design as a college student, my passion was nurtured by a number of gifted teachers, especially Hope Foote at the University of Washington. Since then, I have owned my own interior design firm and shop in San Francisco for more than thirty years, and I still love the challenge of making spaces work for the people who live in them. Over the years, I've distilled what I've learned into twenty-one simple principles that you can use, whatever size house and budget you have. Fortunately, imagination and daring don't cost anything, and these principles can guide you in creating a beautiful home that reflects who you are—no matter where you live.

In this book you will find pictures of beautiful rooms—from my home and from homes my firm has designed. David Wakely, who has been photographing my work for ten years, has a knack for framing the image that captures the essence of a room, or a moment, or a scene. I have also included a number of David's nature photographs. Let them inspire you to open up to the wonders of the world outside your door and to reproduce that beauty in your home.

Your home is your corner of the world. It should both enrich your life and enable you to share your gifts with others. Designing your space is all about who you are and what you enjoy. My hope, in writing this book, is to inspire you to use home design—something we all must do in one fashion or another—as a means of creative self-expression.

Be bold. Think like a three-year-old. Enjoy, have fun.

LOOKING INSIDE

What lies behind us and what lies before us are tiny matters, compared to what lies within us.
—RALPH WALDO EMERSON

Home is shelter from the world: the hearth that warms you, the roof that keeps out the rain, the table where you eat with your loved ones, the bed on which you sleep. But home is also the springboard for your life's adventures and the safety net that gives you courage to soar into the world. At home you are most fully yourself: accepted for the least you are, yet reminded of the most you hope to be.

Putting together a living space that reflects and supports the quest for an authentic life is an exhilarating creative challenge. Begin by looking inside yourself, at your hopes and longings, your needs and fears . . . at the past that shaped you, the present you live in, and the future you yearn for. Then begin to reinvent your home with three simple principles: Weed out unnecessary possessions. Give fresh life to the furnishings you've tired of by moving them around. Stop being frustrated by the physical limitations of your home and start looking for ways to highlight their charms.

A space that meets the everyday needs of its inhabitants, gives expression to their interior life, and encourages them to live the life they want is a glorious thing. The project of creating such a home for yourself can be a source of satisfaction and joy.

1 Edit what you have

When I work on a space, I like to begin by culling the objects in it down to a group of essential items, each of which has a role in meeting the needs of the inhabitants and has found a place in the overall scheme of the household.

Left: This apartment in San Francisco consolidates furnishings from three different residences—a cottage in Carmel, a high-rise pied-à-terre, and a loft-like space in Manhattan—into one home. One-third of the walls were removed, opening up the space so that a variety of forms and attitudes had room in which to meld together gracefully. Some redundant items earned a spot in the new place by finding new roles: This coffee table, before its legs were cut down, was a dining table in the cottage.

Right: Five children and three dogs belong to the family living here. The dogs collect bones, and everyone else collects one thing or another. Their house, with so many collections that can easily overwhelm it, requires constant editing. If this room didn't have the books pushed forward on the shelves, the objects grouped and stacked, and the strong verticals of the bookcases and the lamps, it would look cluttered.

Next spread: The chessboard mounted on the wall of this hallway is from a set whose pieces are characters from *Alice in Wonderland.* The woman who owned this set seldom used it; she confessed that her pleasure came from looking at the figures. So I suggested mounting the board on the wall and displaying the pieces underneath, both to create interest in the hall and to reduce congestion in another area of the apartment that was already crowded with other things.

Editing

In the garden, pruning is as important as cultivation. The same is true in your home. You will enjoy your things more if you constantly edit them, getting rid of what you don't use. Every few years, set up four big boxes labeled "Throw Out," "Give Away," "Pack Away," and "Repair," then go through your closets and drawers and start pruning. Ask yourself: Do I use this regularly? Does it make my life better? The things that don't score a Yes on either question will be easy to toss out or donate to Goodwill. The more difficult choices surround the things you no longer use but are nonetheless reluctant to part with. Here is where discipline comes in: You must choose one of the four boxes! Put all the tools and appliances that need just one little repair in a box and date it. If you haven't dealt with the Repair box in three months, drop the contents off at the next garage sale you run across. The Pack Away box is for everything you're keeping for sentimental reasons—the dress, two sizes too small and fifteen years out of date, that you were wearing when your husband proposed; the trophies that no longer score. Photograph everything, and then pack the box away in the back corner of the cellar or the garage—or give it to your children. Look at the pictures when you want to reminisce.

2 Rearrange things

Even a room that works perfectly and looks great may seem stale after a time. If you never move things around, pretty soon you stop seeing what's there. You can make a space feel dramatically fresh and new—without buying a single new thing or touching a drop of paint—by simply rearranging the objects in it.

Some pieces of furniture, of course, can only be in a particular spot. The piano needs to be away from the heating vent. You want straight lines to run parallel to walls. But for the most part, things can live happily in more than one spot in a room.

Left: People rearrange the chairs in the Luxembourg Gardens in Paris all day long to suit their different needs. When all the people have gone home for the evening, the chairs are still talking to each other.

The two photographs here show one room arranged in two different ways. The sofa and the screen behind it are placed on the only wall that can accommodate them, but everything else is moveable.

Left: Some differences between the two arrangements are subtle. In this view, the candleholder can face the sofa or it can face into the room. The two plants can both be underneath the coffee table, as they are here, or one can rest on top and the other below.

Right: The Cambodian drum that was in the right-hand corner of the room in the shot on the left has become the coffee table here. The glass-topped coffee table is in the back left-hand corner of the room, acting as a support system for a big piece of art that usually hangs in the hall. That drawing is like a Christmas tree—very special and very big—and you might not want it in the same place all the time. Resting it on the table is a better temporary solution than hanging it on the wall.

3 Make the most of limitations

Designers love limitations. They challenge our ingenuity and often push us to find solutions that are even better than what would have been done without any constraints.

Right: This attic room succeeds brilliantly at making the most of its small space. The sofa, a floating shelf suspended thirteen inches above the floor, allows you to see through to the wall as you ascend the stairs and leaves room for storage beneath it. Under the pitched ceiling, the strong horizontal of the built-in running from wall to wall at the far end, repeated in the line of the table, makes the area seem bigger and wider. We have used this ottoman continuously since my associate Helen Craddick designed it in the 1950s, because it accommodates people so comfortably and always makes a minimal space look larger.

Bringing the Outside In

While moving through our hectic days, we can all too easily forget that our lives are bigger than the narrow routine of duty and habit. To climb out of this soulless rut, we need to seek out experiences that help us to remember the exciting vastness of the world outside. To keep from falling back in, we need to bring reminders of these restorative adventures into our homes.

When you take a long walk outdoors, you can drink in the wondrous scale and complexity of the natural world. Observe the sunlight filtered through a canopy of evergreens, the sumptuous texture of a newly plowed field, the complex colors of a beach at dawn. Then re-create these bursts of beauty in your home. Make the vista outside your window a piece of the bedroom. Create a filtered lighting effect in one corner of the study. Paint your dining room the color of the ocean at daybreak.

Travel is a reminder that life can be different. Noses to the grindstone, we begin to believe that the path we're on is the only choice. Go to a different country—or to a different part of your own—and you will remember how varied the world is. When you return home, be sure to keep that sense of possibility alive. Capture the peace of an afternoon in Tuscany by painting a wall in your living room a rich shade of terra-cotta. Savor again the excitement of your stay in Paris as you walk to your front door on a cobblestone path. Bring the outside in.

4 Invite nature inside

Whenever you pull a view inside, the room feels larger and looks better. Think of your windows as being links, rather than barriers.

Left: Placing the flower and log in front of this window opens up a visual connection between the room and the view outside. You can claim the world outside your window, make it a part of your space, with this simple trick.

Left: In this photograph you are looking at a reflection. The mirror, by bringing the view from the window inside, both expands and lightens the interior of this small, dark room.

Right: This shot of a city apartment proves that there is no reason you can't feel as if you live in the country, no matter where you are. The framed botanical prints reinforce the link between the kitchen and the plants outside.

Next page: Here is one of the world's smallest bathrooms, made from a closet off the kitchen. I needed to capture the vista of the garden outside, which I did with a mirror. Notice how the mirror is also the splash—if you divided the mirror from the counter-top you would diminish the sense of scale. Although this room is truly tiny, the view makes it work.

There's a big wonderful world outside your windows, and my belief is that you should borrow as much of it as you possibly can. When we first moved to San Francisco, my wife, Mary, and I lived next to the Presidio, a vast, open green space. We tried in every way imaginable to make the breathtaking scene outside our windows a part of our space. My favorite effect was the row of yellow chrysanthemums growing in five 10-inch pots mounted on freestanding supports outside the dining room: It was enchanting when the window's reflection of the bright line of flowers seem to float on the field of leaves and trees outside. As a result, that compact home with its limited space was probably the most expansive place we've ever lived.

Borrowing

Claim the view outside your window by breaking down the barrier between interior and exterior. If you have a bush with white flowers outside your window, place an arrangement of clippings on the table directly in front of it. That visual connection brings the view inside, creating the feeling of a much larger room.

Make your neighbor's property blend into your yard so that it feels bigger. See if you can plant a climbing rose on the other side of the garden wall so that it can grow and spill over the top. Cover the face of your fence with clinging vines, or paint it out the color of the bark on the trees next door, thus erasing the divide between the two spaces. If climate permits, panel your fence with mirrors to reflect your own space and double its visual depth.

5 Let nature and travel inspire the colors in your home

When you re-create the colors of your favorite places, from both the natural and civilized worlds, you gain unending pleasure—from the beauty of the tones and the warmth of the memories they call forth.

Left and right: Mother Nature is our best teacher. Observe the richness and variety of her neutral palette in these beach rocks. If you take a close look at the pebbles, which at first glance all appear to be beige and brown, you'll see there's an element of red running through them, which you can also see in the edge of the chip in the stone at the top. The interior pictured here assembles the same subtle repetitions that you see in the pattern of the stones.

Left and right: There is a sense of mystery in this very small room, part of a warehouse complex in San Francisco. A dense banana grove planted in the tiny sheltered garden outside is reflected in the walls and ceiling, which are covered with seven layers of blue lacquer. Thick glass shelves are mounted directly into the plaster walls— a magnificent extravagance in earthquake country. Being in this space, which changes as the wind blows, is like floating underwater.

Left: One way to have bright colors in your life is to use them sparingly against a neutral background.

Next page: The people who live in this space are in the travel business and what they bring home shows it. Bright red Oriental lacquer on the walls unites their varied collections. The strong architectural elements of the room allow it to support such an intense color.

Everything has color. If you walk into a white room wearing red, parts of the room will blush pink—just as when you hold a buttercup under your chin, you glow yellow. Color is magical, but you have to control it with a few simple techniques.

Repetition is the key to the effective use of color. If you take some of the ceiling color down into the room, it unifies the room and almost always makes it appear larger. You can also create transitions by taking color from one room and carrying it into the next. If you were a guest at an old-world country mansion, it would be delightful to walk through the green room and the red room and then the white room to get to the gold room, where cocktails were being served. But those of us who live on a somewhat smaller scale need fewer bold contrasts in color. If you want a color to recede, use more of it. Suppose you move into a new house and you hate the carpet, but you take a peek and there's only plywood underneath it. The carpet is brand new, perfectly serviceable, and you really need to spend your money on a new sofa. What you should do is repeat a variation of the carpet color throughout the house so that the carpet recedes. Carry the color up a wall and mount a framed print against it—you'll see the art before you see the wall or the carpet.

I am inclined in general to use neutrals and then work with texture and light to create color, because we all tire of bright, intense tones much faster than we do subdued ones. On the other hand, don't be afraid of rich color—just learn to use it judiciously. A room with a lot of architectural volume absorbs the heat of bold colors well. If you live in a tract house, however, and you paint the plain flat walls of your dining room an intense hot shade, you might find that you'll never again want to serve anything but salads because the room will always seem too warm!

Color

Collect shadows, textures, and reflections

Rather than allowing shadows, textures, and reflections to accumulate haphazardly, you should collect them deliberately. As you compose a room, look for the shadows objects cast, for the variety of ways in which different textures trap the light, and for the many reflections a polished surface can create. Use lights to create or emphasize effects that please you. When these design elements are thoughtfully handled, they can have as much impact in a room as the furnishings do.

Left: I love the play of texture and light in a newly plowed field. The part where the dirt has been turned over is dark, the other part is light, and suddenly you can imagine bright tender green leaves beginning to sprout in those rows. It's the contrast of light and dark that creates interest and complexity.

Right: This I-beam pedestal supports an ancient weather vane. The rooster is great, but the shadow really gives it strength and allows the piece to claim its space in the room. If you look closely at the base that supports the bird, you can see what happens in every room, on every form. One side is darker than the other, and the top, though varied, is lighter than the sides. With fabric, carpet, or any textured materials, it is this opposition of high and low—the contrasting weave, the depth of the pile, the shadow—that makes a room seem rich.

Left: A varied palette of shadows, textures, and reflections animates this corner: the luster of the bronze table, the highlight of the black lacquer underneath the steel weight, the light emphasizing the eyes of the Chinese sculpture on the shelf, the small shadow of the Japanese beast, next to it the semi-concealed spotlight shining on the hardware of the red leather chest, the rich patina of the hand-peeled frame of the chair, the warmth of the hand-woven wool upholstery on the sofa and the textured sofa cushion. This spot says, "Sit back, relax, enjoy." And if you do, in a short time the light from outside will change all the patterns and add another dimension.

7 Find a light for every purpose

There are many kinds of light—reflected, filtered, direct, indirect—and you want to have as much variety as you can. Lamps can be boring. I prefer to have a number of fixtures in various locations so that you get light coming from different directions. Don't forget natural light. Too many people treat a window as a mere hole in the wall; it's much more satisfying to think of the window, and the light that comes through it, as an integral part of the room.

Right: Inspiration is all around you—observe and reinvent for yourself.

Left: You can see a variety of effects in this lovely room. Almost unseen, a direct down-light glows near the connecting point of love seat and sofa. Light from an invisible source highlights the top of the basket, and the dramatically strong pylon in the far corner throws 300 watts onto the ceiling. Late afternoon light comes through all the windows, which will show outdoor illumination after dark.

Right: The lighting in this loft by architect Ira Kurtlander is fairly obvious, and not only for dramatic impact—there was no way to hide it. It's like a stage set without a scrim or wings. Everything is exposed, including the theatrical light shining on the canvas to the left and the spots shining on the floor. The floor is concrete, textured and polished to look like granite, and the light from above gives it luster.

Next page: Here, light glows on the chipped gesso of the Chinese form and bounces off the Indian bronze pot and the wee pre-Columbian head. Looking at this photo, I'm transported to the moment at the end of a long day, when I'm in the living room with a friendly glass of port, and I get a chance to remember buying the small sculpture in Amsterdam. I'm charmed by the memory and enchanted by the light—the light on the floor behind the sculpture, the light from the floor lamp purposely illuminating the flowers. The port's glowing (or I'm glowing because of the port), and it's magic.

The best examples of light come from two opposite extremes: from the untouched corners of the natural world and from the theater, the height of artifice. If you can incorporate some effects from both in lighting your home—filtered sunlight through a louvered shade, alongside dramatic uplighting from a floor spot—you will have something really special.

Light

Lighting should be organized so that you notice the illumination, not the source. I don't like fixtures that dingle-dangle from the middle of the ceiling. I would rather use something so large that you don't see it. In 1950, Gross Wood designed a pan light like a plow disk—36 inches across and $7\frac{1}{2}$ inches total depth from the ceiling, with three 150-watt bulbs—that is still available today. When you look up to the ceiling with this treatment you don't see a light fixture, you see a moon out in space.

A host of problems can be solved with lighting. If the ceiling needs painting but you don't want to spend the money on that right now, you can place a light on the floor, hugging the side of a pot filled with tall branches, to make a shadow on the ceiling that disguises the cracks. If your sofa is slightly soiled but you want to wait to buy a new one, pull it away from the wall a few inches (put a couple of blocks behind the legs so it doesn't slip back) and put lighting behind the sofa. The sofa is seen in shadow now and doesn't look soiled.

8 Build a room outdoors

You can put some furniture in your backyard, or you can construct outdoor rooms from which you will get unending pleasure. Europeans know how to do this, but North Americans have forgotten how to use walls outside. Places like Versailles have intimate corners within the framework of a great public space. You can learn how to bring that kind of complexity into your 12-foot-square plot. There are all kinds of joy to be had in the intimate use of light, space, and the sound of water—and you don't have to hire an army of gardeners!

Left: In this garden room, on a rooftop above a garage, every single plant is growing in a pot. The slate is very pretty in this shot, but it's fabulous when the garden is filled with fog or when the plants have just been watered and every cloud up above is reflected in it.

Left: Here's another view of the rooftop garden on page 57. The flow of space gives you a sense of wandering through a wood, as the garden is divided into three rooms.

Top right: In this wonderful outdoor room, notice how the lines of the table match the lines of the deck, and how the railings, spaced according to the building code, blend into the backs of the benches.

Bottom right: When this garden was first developed, the owners had two dogs that needed a separate space. So I created a sculpture garden with gravel on the ground for the dogs and separated the people's area from the animals' with a bench. It's long, accommodating two 6-foot seating pads, sculpture, trees, and cutout spaces for smaller greenery.

Many people use water to cover up the sounds of urban conversation—fire engines, garbage trucks, jack hammers—but water can also be invaluable in the suburbs. To absorb the sound of a freeway, you need two hundred feet of thicket. If you don't have enough room, you can mask the sound quite effectively with a fountain. Or, you can create an illusion with two or three feet of bamboo massed so tightly you trick people into thinking that they shouldn't hear the noise through such a barrier—and so they don't.

Left: An outdoor room makes an interior space appear bigger than it really is. This bedroom looks out on the yard in two places. The piece of wall between the two doors could easily have been a barrier to the outside, but the strong white lines, the thick glass shelves seeming to float within them, and the mirror at the back allow the two garden views to flow into each other.

Right: Anyone can have a fountain—this is a homemade one, created from redwood rubbed with baking soda to give it a rich patina.

Memory and the Things You Love

You truly claim your living space and make it your own when you display the things you love. Artworks, souvenirs from your travels, simple mementos of significant days—all these bits and pieces from your past declare, as nothing else in your home can, "This is who I am."

Each one of your valued objects tells two stories. The smooth gray stone resting on your end table tells your guests that you love to walk on the beach and that you have an eye for natural beauty. But the stone tells another story, for you alone: the memory of the winter sun, glinting on the whitecapped water; the cries of the gulls; the cold sand between your bare toes; and the weight of your friend's arm on your shoulder.

Collections begin when you take the things you love and arrange them in a way that is beautiful. Once I worked with someone who was the grandson of a craftsman. He had his grandfather's tools—twenty-four hand-made wooden planes—stored in the garage. They didn't belong in the garage! Once they were spruced up, mounted, and displayed, they covered an entire wall. That fellow now has a significant collection of beautiful forms to grace his home. He also has a durable shrine that not only honors his grandfather but also recalls him. It's not what you have, it's what you *do* with what you have that's important.

9 Display the things you love

You should handle your displays the way you handle your friends. If you find a new friend, you don't tell your old friend, "Sorry, I have a new friend, so I have no time for you." You make room for the new friend while continuing to treasure the old one, finding the right spot in your life for each. If you look closely at the wall in this photograph, you will see small holes from places where something was moved to make room for an addition to this collection.

Left: I love the forms of African sculptures, although I can't afford to own them. But I do have a lot of old tools, so I display them as a collection of forms. Notice how the strong terra-cotta background color pulls the group together, making of it a whole that demands closer attention.

Left: These shelves are glass, resting on rods, and the bottoms have been sandblasted so the dust won't show. Notice how each of these items has room to spread its wings, how none of them is lined up in a straight row. Rather, they are grouped like friends in conversation.

Top right: If you display an illustrated book open on a table, you have more time to absorb its beauty. Turn a page every day or two and you will have a new experience of the book.

Bottom right: Consider painting the back of your bookshelf a rich color. Many book bindings are dark blue or red, so when there is a deep color behind them it is not as evident that some books are in good condition and some aren't, or that some are small and some are big. And if you bring all the books forward so that the spines sit on the front of the shelf there is less room for dust to collect.

Next page: Even humble everyday items, organized with care and displayed with grace, can become a lovely collection.

Possessions have a way of becoming a great part of your life, and they enrich a home. Clutter, however, is the enemy of a beautiful home. You can have as many possessions as you want, but it shouldn't appear that you have too many. When you invest some thought and care into how your objects will be displayed, you transform a jumble of things into an attractive collection.

Collections

You can mount superb pieces on a stark white background, as some museums do. But if your things aren't all absolutely exquisite, their flaws will be very evident. Instead, use a softer background color. The same technique works well in subduing a room that has too many objects. My wife, Mary, and I travel quite a bit. A few years ago we found that our collections were beginning to take over our house. When we painted our white walls a soft golden color, our things became less overwhelming visually. So we were able to continue acquiring more and more on our trips.

Some things can stand alone, and others need a lot of friends. Often, you might have one thing that is really great and two other items that aren't so wonderful—but for one reason or another you love them all. Group the three together, which takes a little bit of importance away from each of the individual items but creates an arrangement in which no object fails to please the eye.

10 Invest
in quality

Quality lasts for a very long time
and is worth a great deal. Don't be
afraid of it.

Left: This Japanese chest is the
equivalent of an entire room. You
could separate the sections, elevating
the upper one and capping the lower
with a slab of marble or granite. Or,
the chest could remain intact and
fill one side of a room from floor to
ceiling and wall to wall. These arm-
chairs are also exquisite: They offer
ease of access and unbelievable
comfort. Everything in this room
is really fine and beautiful: the
Japanese drum used as an end table,
the Celtic figure suspended on a
trapeze, even the three many-times-
repaired washtubs from Korea that
rest on the top of the tansu along
with the grain measure from China.
This is a room with style, and it
doesn't know what vogue is.

Left: When you respect something enough to frame it decently, you bestow dignity on even a childish drawing. I like to center a picture between two sheets of glass, so that the background color of the wall becomes the mat.

Right: Many everyday activities can be a lot nicer if you go to only a little extra trouble and get yourself beautiful and well-made equipment.

Next spread: A young craftsman came to me with an exact reproduction of a High Wycombe chair. Over the next three years, as I continued to buy chairs from him, I asked if he could change it a little bit here and there, getting rid of the detailing on the legs, cutting down the dimple on the seat, adding bamboo shoots to support the joinery. Two hundred years from now someone should still be using this marvelous chair, which is comfortable to sit on and beautiful to look at, handmade by a craftsman who learned his trade in Japan, perfected it in High Wycombe, and produced his masterpiece in the United States.

Quality

Quality shows in simplicity of line, excellence of construction, and ease of movement. A good sofa has a great frame that shows its simple well-defined lines from all four sides. It's long enough so that you can fit between the arms when you want to take a nap and comfortable enough that when someone tosses a blanket over you and you don't wake up until the next morning you've had a good night's sleep. The sofa in my living room has been covered in the same fabric, natural hand-woven wool, for more than twenty-five years, and it's still good.

With true quality, you might pay more than you think you can afford, but you'll be able to live with it the rest of your life. In today's marketplace, you could easily spend the same amount of money on a few good things as you would on a bunch of items that fill your space with mediocrity and need to be replaced every few years.

I encourage people to buy things for their homes that will last, things they can pass on to their children. Recently I was talking to someone about building a piece of furniture and I said, "This bookcase is going to be so good that some day a little girl will say, 'My great-grandmother had this made.'" So this frugal woman commissioned something for someone she may never see. That's quality.

One of the most expensive things I own is a print by an artist named Glen Alps, who was a superb teacher at the University of Washington when I studied there. I didn't have a lot of money in those student days, so I spent three Saturdays in a row mixing clay for the school's ceramics studio to earn $75 to buy the piece; it took me two years after that to save enough to frame it. That picture still holds a place of honor in my home. Whenever I walk by it now, more than fifty years later, I am reminded of the promise of those youthful times, and my teacher and friend.

Always find a way to get quality. It's more than worth the effort.

11 Realize that something special is often very simple

Living amid so much abundance, we can easily begin to think that every aspect of our lives needs its own specialized gadget. Savor the beauty of the simple things that already surround you and the joy to be had in adapting objects at hand to new uses.

Left: This stone hasn't been used for grinding meal in a long time. Now it collects water and the odd coin or two. Allowing it to acquire a patina of algae enhances its charm.

Right: A bouquet from a home garden is the most expensive floral arrangement you can have. Masses of blossoms from the florist, whatever you pay for them, could never be as rewarding as the bunch of roses your friend cultivated, fed, watered, and then brought to you.

12 Look at the space around an object

Often, it is the space between the objects that holds a successful arrangement together.

Left: Notice how the tiny pre-Columbian whistle, shaped like a head, is brought close to the Indian pot. The African sculpture is placed just close enough to the Japanese plate to create a tension between them.

Right: I love the diversity of objects in this arrangement. Each of them—the tool in the foreground, the flax comb resting on a metal stand behind it, the bocce ball to the right, and the decoys to the left—has found a spot that's just right in relationship to the others.

Next spread: Too many small things made this display look cluttered. When I improvised a stand for the figure next to the lamp, making it bigger and bolder, the tabletop came together.

Placement

One of the most memorable assignments I was given as an architecture student was to get a ream of plain white paper and to place a black dot on each of those 8½-by-11 sheets: one dot per page, never in the same place. Once I'd done that to every one of those five hundred sheets, I had to go back and select the best-looking page. The majority of the seventy students in the class agreed that the most successful placements put the dot on the top half of the page, closer to the right edge than the left, with the distances from all four edges of varying lengths. That dot has been with me constantly since then. It is the key to placing a house on a property, trees in a garden, a lamp on a table, food on a plate.

Often the space around an object is as important as the object itself. If you have a collection, don't line the pieces up, one after another in a row, with equal spaces in between. Play with the distances so that, in the end, one object rests with another and is complemented by yet another. Have you ever seen someone wearing a piece of jewelry and wondered, "How *did* she manage to find the spot that makes that pin look just right?" She did it by standing in front of a mirror and trying it first in one place, and then in another and another, until she happened on the location that was perfect. You can too.

Discover
new ways
to store things

Finding new ways to store things is one of the most creative things you can do in your home. Stretch your imagination and find objects that are beautiful in themselves to use as storage containers.

Left: To me, this large metal grain container looks like a great African sculpture. When I first bought it, the jar was purely decorative, but now I put my dirty shirts in it.

Top right: I knew a young man who would buy brown eggs at the market, put them in a basket filled with straw, and then go door to door to sell them. People would look at his tanned face, the kerchief around his neck, and his overalls and they would say, "Oh, Tommy, your eggs are always so fresh!" You can have a cardboard box of eggs or you can have a collection of eggs in a basket in your refrigerator. Which do you think looks more inviting?

Lower right: A Shaker box is an excellent example of an object that is both beautiful and practical as storage. Here, one holds old photographs. On one of the shelves above it you can see an intriguing box that does double duty as a bookend, while the shelf below stores an entire troupe of French bicyclists.

Next page: One Japanese tansu topped with granite sits on the floor. Another is lifted closer to the ceiling (but still within easy reach) and lighting has been installed underneath it. The chests provide plenty of storage and give the room lots of warmth.

When people think about storage, they tend to think "closets," many of which are inefficient and awkward. I find that opening a closet up from wall to wall and floor to ceiling can help, but occasionally I will go even further and just eliminate it. Once you've done that you can fill the space with a piece of furniture. I enjoy using Japanese tansu, double chests that can fit side by side or stack. If you take a large one and separate the top from the bottom, suspend the top piece close to the ceiling with floating lights underneath it, and top the bottom with a new hard surface, you end up with a room that looks larger and offers more storage than you had before the closet was removed.

Storage

Some of the very best storage is visible, like a wooden bowl brimming with the potatoes you're going to cook for dinner tonight or a chest filled with rolls and rolls of brilliantly colored ribbons. I love to recreate the effect of an old-fashioned country general store, in which a bounty of tempting things—coffee beans, penny candies, whole grains—is visible behind panes of glass.

If you think about it, you'll realize that you have storage spaces throughout your house, from the rubber bands around the kitchen door-knob to the stacks of towels in the linen closet. With a bit of imagination and effort, every one of them can become a really pretty spot.

> Cartons are houses for crackers.
> Castles are houses for kings.
> The more that I think about houses
> The more things are houses for things.
>
> —MARY ANNE HOBERMAN,
> *A House Is a House for Me*

THE POETICS OF HOME

Interior design, like all arts, is a complex blend of related elements—rhythm, balance, texture, color, and repetition—that tend to be invisible in a successful space. An elegantly appointed, well-edited room has a quiet and deeply pleasing flow. When you first walk in, just as when you stumble upon an exquisite spot in the forest, you can't identify precisely what you find so satisfying—nor do you particularly want to. You simply accept the gift of its charm.

If you want to truly understand the poetics of home, think about a wonderful party. The hosts bring forward the best they have to offer: music, food, drink, flowers, sculpture, glassware, lighting. The spirit of generosity and excitement creates an electric spark in the air. Forms appear sublime; the conversation seems brilliant, and the laughter joyous. If you were to try, the morning after, to analyze the success of the evening you would decide that the magical whole far exceeded the sum of its parts.

That alchemy is only possible because of the ongoing attention the hosts devote to the arrangement of their home. Spaces that allow people to gather and flow, that please the eye, and create a sense of ease do not happen overnight. They result from the careful consideration of a hundred questions: Can we make the boundary between the dining room and the living room disappear? Does this area have a focal point? How does everything in this space work together?

Like the skeleton of a high rise or the rhyme scheme of a sonnet, this imperceptible yet essential foundation is what makes the creation of a beautiful home possible.

Create
focal points
for each room

Every room needs up to three focal
points, of decreasing weight, so that
your eye knows to go first here, then
there, then there. If a space has only
one very strong focal point, you see
too much at once. You want to leave
some mystery intact, some secrets
that aren't revealed at first glance.

Right: Views are often obvious focal
points, but sometimes you need to
improve them. Here, a huge bay
replaced short, viewless windows.
In one direction, it looks out to the
Golden Gate Bridge, but the house
next door is what you see in the
other direction. I mirrored the
side panel on that side of the bay
window so that the view of the
neighbor's home was replaced by
a reflection of the bridge view.

Left: The entryway to our apartment is quite formal. The chest at the back is centered, the coach lamps flank the door, the columns are symmetrical, and the mirror instantly commands attention. When it's party time, flowers and candles, placed off center, set a less formal welcoming tone.

Top right: Here, the original fireplace remains as a strong focal point, but some of its dominance is taken away by the vertical lines of the columns that were added as support when the doorway and a wall were removed.

Bottom right: A fireplace is a natural focal point. If you don't have one, you can create the same kind of impact with an arrangement of furniture or, in this case, a fireplace cover resting on a floating shelf.

 Buy furniture
that is flexible

For a flexible piece of furniture—
something you can use in different
places for multiple functions—a
chair is hard to beat. A comfortable
chair is priceless. Often, if a chair
is not comfortable to sit in for long
periods of time, it is because the
pitch of the seat is not quite right.
If you find that you are sliding
forward, try experimenting with the
angle of the seat, raising the front
legs incrementally by propping a
layer of magazines underneath them.
When you have found the right
pitch, measure the depth of the shim
and have a carpenter cut that much
off the back legs.

Left: These black University chairs
designed by Ward Bennett can be
used in any room in the house. Now
lined up at a desk against the wall,
they can instantly be moved to the
table and serve as dining chairs.

Right: This daybed is made up of a mattress and box spring upholstered in a nice fabric that is channel-quilted on top to prevent wrinkling. It's extremely comfortable for sleeping and makes a wonderful sofa. If you stored some sheets, blankets, and pillows in the cabinet, your spare bedroom could be ready in a couple of minutes—as soon as you emptied the Shaker pegs on the wall for your guest's use and made up the bed.

When my wife and I lived in a house with a very small dining space, we worked wonders with an ever-changing arrangement of tables and chairs. We bought a gate-leg table and a pair of consoles that could make a single 42-inch round table. The consoles could also be attached to one or both ends of the drop-leaf table—which could be closed, half-open, or fully open. We now have a generously sized dining room that allows us even greater flexibility with the same furniture.

Left: Here we put the consoles on either side of the opened drop-leaf table and covered everything with four pie-shaped leaves. The resulting round table is seven feet across. It is perfect for a dinner party for twelve. The plant stand supports flowers above everyone's head so that conversation can reign.

Right: Another view, another time. The 42-inch-wide table is supporting five table leaves that rest on top, enlarging the surface to nearly five feet wide and ten feet long. The kilim on top makes me feel as if I'm having a meal in a Vermeer painting.

16 Work with illusion and scale to alter your space

Scale is one of the most important elements of interior design. It involves line and proportion as well as height and mass. Big things in small spaces can create a sense of expansiveness; small things in big rooms can carve out an intimate space.

Left: When I look at the wonderful Medici Fountain in Paris, I cannot help but try to figure out how to convert its brilliant illusions into ideas that can work similar miracles for me. The fountain bed narrows toward the back, creating the impression of great distance. The surface underneath the water also slants up as it goes toward the front, and the perspective created by the apparent drop in the level of the water at the back bestows more grandeur on the fountain than its actual dimensions would allow.

Top left: Here, the curtains have been stripped away so that the mirrors, installed from wall to wall, become the window treatment. That wall creates a feeling of space and light that would normally be impossible to achieve in a room of this size.

Bottom left: The back of this gazebo is mirrored to screen off a view of the tool shed and a neighbor's house. Having the reflected view of the house and garden as a backdrop fosters a sense of privacy as well as spaciousness.

Right: This is a small bathroom, so I wanted to move the eye around the room. I used mirrors—the one you see in this photograph reflects itself three times. I also used long lines. Notice how the white shade (reflected in the mirror on the left-hand side of the photo) covering the bathtub goes all the way to the floor. You could use the same trick to put off remodeling if you've changed the décor of your bathroom and the tile no longer matches. Just cover it up instead of replacing it.

Left: This cabinet is in a room with 10-foot ceilings. The height of the cabinet makes your eye travel all the way to the ceiling, which makes the room appear larger.

Right: The small scale of this tabletop display, drawing you in to look at it closely, creates a sense of intimate immensity in a vast entrance hall.

A successful transition creates a pleasing flow from one space to the other.

Left: Here, an anteroom with a skylight for a ceiling was created by walling off an area in front of the house. Closed, the louvered doors provide privacy without sacrificing air or light. Opened, they beckon guests to the front door.

Right: Color and function unite these two spaces. The hallway has been painted the same color as the interior of the English pine cabinet. The white handles on the black kitchen doors pick up the white ironstone in the cabinet. You can't be sure where one room ends and the other begins; the space appears much larger as a result.

Next page: Removing doors and walls opened up this hallway so that it relates better to the addition in the back.

To control the biggest transition, from outside to inside, you have to think about dirt and how it affects flooring. If you have a white carpet in the living room and right outside there's a deck leading to a garden covered in peat moss, that carpet is going to be dirty all the time. Smooth dark surfaces can be equally unforgiving, showing dust and dog hair right away. The grain of a wood floor can hide soil, just as a high/low texture in carpet or upholstery fabric does. An Oriental rug is perfect for the dining room, since the spots from cranberry sauce and gravy never show. For the same reason I like to use a kilim as a tablecloth for dinner parties (although I do confess that I keep the salt cellar near at hand so that I don't have to break off an interesting conversation if I happen to knock over the wine). But some places, like bath and kitchen counters, need to show dirt right away so that it can be easily seen and removed.

Dirt

You can use a number of things to keep too much of the outdoors from coming in: large front door mats, foot scrapers out back, outdoor showers. Invest in these and you will be able to spend all the time you would have spent cleaning doing something much more interesting.

18 Plan a kitchen that helps you cook

I have worked on superb kitchens, and they're usually very plain. Often, when people go into a kitchen shop, the salesperson will say, "Do you want French Provincial or American Colonial?" That's really foolish. The kitchen should be a serviceable place that's easy to clean, with as much light as possible and wide counter tops. I advise people who are planning kitchen remodels to work through an entire recipe, taking notes as they go, so that they have a detailed idea of what their kitchen needs to do for them.

Left: This is kitchen as theater, the stage for a great dinner. The twelve Ward Bennett chairs are set around the dining table when there's a big party afoot, but they are placed throughout the loft at other times. The long table is on wheels and can be split into sections and moved out of the room when there's no need to seat so many people.

Left: Look at the thickness of these countertops, the warmth of the lighting in the ceiling and under the cabinets, the mirror repeating the space and light. Even when it's cluttered, this kitchen looks clean.

Top right: There's a wonderful ease in the flow between the cooking and dining areas here. The utilitarian lines and neutral colors make the kitchen feel clean, but the warmth of the wood table and the sunshine keep it from seeming sterile.

Bottom right: These cabinets open both ways, so you can reach for dishes from either the kitchen or the dining room. Notice how the brightness of the honed marble on the countertops is echoed in the tile on the splash and in those nice porcelain knobs.

 Design children's
rooms to expand
with their
imaginations

The secret to coming up with a good
room for a child is respect. For
example, if you take a drawing by
a child and stick it on the refrigerator
among a bunch of other things,
nobody will think of it as being
anything special. But if you have
a few plastic frames in the bathroom and you regularly change the
drawings you display in them, your
child will know that the work is
outstanding and much loved.

Right: Any child would find this
furniture useful and appropriate for
many years. There's nothing better
than a high-backed wing chair for
a kid's room, because it invites so
many different relaxing poses. The
suitcases stacked in the corner are
filled with all kinds of treasures.

Next page: A room can preserve
pieces of a child's past at the same
time that it keeps pace with a
teenager's present-day needs.

When I was twelve, my parents built a new house. Once they had established a budget for my room, the woman who worked on the new place interviewed me about my tastes and needs, and we thought about possibilities together. I ended up with some things that I was willing to live with forever, like the cabinet, complete with ice bucket and glasses, from which I could serve my friends Cokes. Can you imagine what that did for my social standing? My room also had a doorknocker. From that experience I learned to include children in the planning of their rooms.

Children

I strongly discourage parents of infants from buying furniture decorated with ABCs or little lambs or other childish themes. Cutie-pie furniture has a short life and a tendency to stay around too long. It's much more satisfying to invest in a decent chest of drawers, a good and timeless piece of furniture that your child will still enjoy in her college dorm—or even in her first apartment. Put the primary colors or blackboard paint on the walls, which will need to be repainted every few years anyway.

Our world is too much organized for adult bodies, adult schedules, and adult tastes. If you want a great light fixture for a child's room, get a big Chinese dragon kite and hang it on the ceiling. Plug in two lines of Christmas tree lights so they go into each section of the dragon and come out the eyes. Adults will have to duck to walk underneath this light, which will delight the people who are only a few feet tall. Garages have huge amounts of space that is empty once the adults have driven to work. But the kid world doesn't stop during the day. Why not equip the garage with tumbling mats and a trampoline and a basketball hoop? The indoor gym can easily disappear into the corners before the cars come home at dinnertime. Try to have one extravagantly child-based feature in your house: a slide from the second story down to the garden, a huge attic play space, a ladder climbing from a bedroom window up to a deck.

 Set aside a place
in which to be
happy alone

We all need a corner where we can
curl up alone yet not feel lonely.
These spots have completely different
moods, but all four invite retreat and
promise to protect solitude.

Right: This fabulous chair, mellow
and weathered, has its own sheltered
place in my garden.

Left: A peaceful corner with a collection of good books encourages contented reflection. I love the texture of this chair and ottoman, the metal rods supporting the hand-hewn shelf, and the lovely view.

Next spread, left: You want to make sure that your window seat isn't too high: The ideal height is actually thirteen inches from the floor. It's also important to have adequate padding as well as something comfortable to rest your back against.

Next spread, right: Soft light, coming from a variety of sources, creates a restful feeling in this charming room.

21 Learn the art of sharing your home

Setting the right tone for a gathering is an art. For a large cocktail party, I'll turn the lights on bright and crank up the show tunes, because I expect people to spend only a few hours with us and we'll all have more fun if the energy level is high. When we're having a dinner party, however, the lights are dimmed and we play soft music, encouraging conversation to run into the wee hours.

Left and right: I love opening our home to friends, and I especially love the preparations: bringing in pots of flowers to mass in the entryway, lining up the gleaming silverware, laying out the candles and stemware.

Right: Here is our living room, a wonderful space. Twenty-four people can gather, half of them standing, to toast a friend's special day. It's always what I want it to be and yet it changes constantly: The headlights of a passing car throw a shadow against the wall. Sunlight reflects differently on the surfaces of the room, depending on the season. The furniture, however, is pretty static. You never need to pull the chairs closer, because they have been placed to make conversation easy. The bench can accommodate three people and allows even more to cluster around it. There is room enough for several people to stand around the piano. At day's end, turning out the lights and pausing to watch the shadows from the lights outside playing on the surfaces of this room is like saying a prayer.

A GOOD ROOM IS NEVER DONE

Creating a room is like making a salad. Ever so delicately, you dip in a finger and find that the dressing needs a bit of salt. Or perhaps it would enjoy a little more lemon. You add some of this and some of that, then you taste again. And so you proceed: tasting repeatedly, adding small pinches of seasonings as you go, until the salad is just right.

It's no different when you design your home. When your space reflects who you are, it alters continually as your life evolves. Occasionally, you face a monumental change that requires a virtual overhaul of your entire space. But more often you keep making the kind of small adjustments you make when you cook.

The elements that keep your home fresh involve continual change. Placing autumn leaves on this table will necessitate moving that sculpture. The Christmas tree coming in means that the chair in the corner must reside elsewhere for a time. If you love the reflection of early morning light on a particular silver plate, you will need to move that piece around to follow the sun throughout the year.

Since I keep my mind open to possibilities—thinking like a three-year-old—my home continues to engage me. I am nearly always absorbed in schemes for refinements, because a good room is never done. Thank goodness! Our lives are enriched by the ongoing delight of making fine things even better. I hope you find as much joy in it as I do.

Page 2 Designer: Siobhàn Brennan; *Sunflower* by Robert Mapplethorpe; *Nude Woman* by Katherine Renfield **Page 8** Designer: John K. Wheatman **Page 11** Designer: Peter L. Gilliam; *The Yellow Paper* by Libby Wadsworth **Page 12** Designer: John K. Wheatman **Page 14** *Oaxacan Monastery* by David Wakely **Pages 16-17** Designer: Siobhàn Brennan; Scissors chairs by Ward Bennett; Lighting by Phoenix Day, Cassella Lighting; Artwork by Mark Petersen; Raku vessels by Bill Kennedy; Television by Bang & Olufsen **Pages 18-19** Designer: John K. Wheatman; Coffee table by McGuire Furniture Co. **Page 21** Designer: Siobhàn Brennan; Chess set by Robin and Nell Dale **Pages 24-25** Designer: John K. Wheatman; Glass-top table and wall vase executed by Roger Yearout; Celtic Man candleholder adapted by John K. Wheatman and executed by Roger Yearout and Frog Hollow Studio; *Threshold* by Susan Manchester; Pottery by Blaine Shirk **Pages 26-27** Designer: Helen Reed Craddick; Chair by Earo Aarnio **Pages 28-29** *Fish Lake* by David Wakely **Pages 32-33** Designer: John K. Wheatman **Page 34** Designer: Peter L. Gilliam; Fixture by Kroin **Page 36** *Point Lobos* by David Wakely **Page 37** Designer: Helen Reed Craddick; *Grapefruit* by Ellsworth Kelly; Chair by Ken Mochi **Page 38** Designer: Jonathan Straley; University chairs by Ward Bennett **Page 39** *Pool Reflections* by David Wakely **Pages 40-41** Designer: Peter Gilliam; *4th Planet Study* by Stan Berning; Barcelona chairs by Mies van der Rohe; Pottery by Blaine Shirk; Celtic Man candleholder adapted by John K. Wheatman and executed by Roger Yearout and Frog Hollow Studio **Page 42** Designer: Jonathan Straley **Page 44** *Furrowed Field* by David Wakely **Pages 46-47** Designer: John K. Wheatman; Chair by McGuire Furniture Co.; Table by Laurence Montano **Pages 48-49** From left to right, *Brescia Dining Room*, *Paris Opera*, and *Pantheon*, by David Wakely **Pages 50-51** Designer: Helen Reed Craddick; Lighting by Gage Cauchois, Casella Lighting; Artwork by Ellsworth Kelly; Cast aluminum sculpture by H. Steinbrenner; *Tour de France* by Louise Burns **Pages 52-53** Designer: Jonathan Straley; Architect: Ira Kurtlander; Chairs by Donghia **Page 54** Designer: John K. Wheatman **Pages 56-57** Designer: John K. Wheatman; Bench and garden wall by Thomas Church; Stained glass by Giovanni Hajnal **Page 58** Designer: John K. Wheatman; Chairs by Robert Mallet-Stevens **Page 59 top** Designer: Helen Reed Craddick; Table by Helen Reed Craddick **Page 59 bottom** Designer: John K. Wheatman; Chairs by Brown-Jordan; Horse sculpture by Mike Moran **Page 60** Designer: John K. Wheatman; *Ginger Cat* by Barbara Spring **Page 61** Fountain design by Helen Reed Craddick **Pages 64-65** Designer: John K. Wheatman **Page 66** Designer: John K. Wheatman **Page 67 top** Designer: Peter L. Gilliam; Lighting by R. Jesse; Table by Gregory Hay, Chairmaker **Page 67 bottom** Designer: John K. Wheatman **Page 68** Designer: John K. Wheatman **Pages 70-71** Designer: John K. Wheatman; Chairs by Geiger-Brickel; Table by Douglas Senft; *Wild River #46* by Geoffrey Williams; Celtic man sculpture adapted by John K. Wheatman and executed by Roger Yearout and Frog Hollow Studio **Page 72** Designer: John K. Wheatman; Drawings by Charles Quillan; *Monkeys* by Giovanni Hajnal; Pottery by Dennis Meiners **Page 75** Chair detailed by John Wheatman with Dennis Young and manufactured by Gregory Hay, Chairmaker **Page 77** Pottery by George Orbelian **Pages 78-79** *Two Drunken Dutchmen* by Augustin Hanicotte (1870-1957) **Page 82** Designer: John K. Wheatman; Vintage snowshoe chair by Abercrombie & Fitch **Page 84** Designer: Jonathan Straley; Chair by McGuire Furniture Co. **Page 87** *Native Instinct* by David Wakely **Pages 88-89** Designer: Jonathan Straley; Chair by Donghia **Page 90** Designer: John K. Wheatman **Page 91 top** Designer: Peter L. Gilliam; Coffee table by McGuire Furniture Co. **Page 91 bottom** Designer: Helen Reed Craddick **Pages 92-93** Designers: John Wheatman & Associates; University chairs by Ward Bennett; Parentisi lamp by Italiana Luce; Photographs by Ruffin Cooper **Pages 94-95** Designer: Helen Reed Craddick; Chairs by Mies van der Rohe; Lighting by Berenice; Stacking futon/daybed by Marco **Pages 96-97** Designer: John K. Wheatman; Dining chairs by Eleanor Forbes for McGuire Furniture Co.; Plant stand by McGuire Furniture Co.; Stained glass by Giovanni Hajnal **Page 100 top** Designer: John K. Wheatman; Dining table and chairs by McGuire Furniture Co. **Page 100 bottom** Designer: Peter L. Gilliam; Garden furniture by Summit Furniture Inc. **Page 101** Designer: John K. Wheatman; Chair by Robert Mallet-Stevens **Page 102** Designer: John K. Wheatman; Officer's chair by Eleanor Forbes for McGuire Furniture Co. **Page 103** Designer: Peter L. Gilliam; Dining table by Ward Bennett; Wall-hung vase by Japonesque **Page 104** Designer: John K. Wheatman; *Frozen* by Cindy Kane; *Balance* by Joe Brubaker **Page 105** Designer: John K. Wheatman **Page 106** Designer: Peter L. Gilliam; Architectural team: Architectural Resources Group, John K. Wheatman and Peter Gilliam **Pages 108-109** Designer: Jonathan Straley; Table by Spaulding Taylor; University chairs by Ward Bennett **Page 110** Designer: Siobhàn Brennan; Stove top and hood by Viking Range Corporation; Kitchen accessories by Alessi **Page 111 top** Designer: Jonathan Straley; Chairs by Ward Bennett **Page 111 bottom** Designer: Peter L. Gilliam; Architects: Architectural Resources Group **Pages 112-113** Designer: John K. Wheatman; Lighting by Robert Long **Page 114** Designer: John K. Wheatman **Page 117** Designer: John K. Wheatman **Page 118** Designer: Peter L. Gilliam **Page 119** Designer: Helen Reed Craddick; Ant chair by Arne Jacobsen; Lighting by Koch & Lowy, Gage Cauchois **Pages 122-123** Designer: John K. Wheatman; Celtic coffee table by John K. Wheatman, executed by Roger Yearout and Frog Hollow Studio; Chairs by McGuire Furniture Co.; Area rug by Carousel

Every effort has been made to credit the artists and artisans whose works figure prominently in the photographs. We apologize for any omissions and would be happy to insert appropriate credits in subsequent editions.

John Wheatman, who was selected as one of *House Beautiful's* Top American Designers in 1999, has had his own design firm in San Francisco for more than 35 years. He has also spent more than 40 years as a lecturer, beginning at Mills College in Oakland, California and now at the University of California at Berkeley's Extension and the Inchbald School of Design in London, England.

David Wakely is a San Francisco-based photographer whose books include *Markets of Provence, A Sense of Mission: Historic Churches of the Southwest, San Francisco: Point of View*, and *Gregorian Chant*. His work has also appeared in many magazines and design journals, including *Interior Design, Architectural Record*, and *Sunset Magazine*. You can find him on the web at www.davidwakely.com.